Grand Central

ANDY BROWN

BRITAIN'S RAILWAYS SERIES, VOLUME 31

Contents page image: 43068, in the original plain black Grand Central livery, leads the 1A61 13.42 Sunderland–King's Cross around the Durham Coast and passes Hawthorn Dene on 7 March 2010. (Dave Stacey)

Acknowledgements

As a lifelong landscape and railway photographer, Grand Central was the natural subject for my first book, given that the company handed me my first railway job, for which I am eternally grateful. Thanks go to the invaluable contributions of the following photographers and contributors, without the assistance of whom this book would not have been possible.

Michael J Alderdice	Mark Delaney	Phil Metcalfe
Alisdair Anderson	Richard Dyke	Sam Middleton
Ian Ball	Will Etherington	Gavin Morrison
Steve Bennett	Terry Eyres	Tom Robson
Scott Borthwick	Neil Gibson	Jason Rogers
Andy Brown	Neil Harrison	Jamie Squibbs
Phil Chilton	Alan Hart	Dave Stacey
Paul Corrie	Neil Harvey	Tom Swift
Alex Cooke	Anthony Hicks	John Turner
Jason Cross	Ian Holmes	Rob Whitaker
Kieren Cross	Jonathon Kirby	Sean English and all at Grand Central
Chris Davis		

The book is dedicated to my son Jack, who loves everything about Grand Central – in his room he has several of my pictures framed, along with a hand-painted mural depicting a Class 180.

Published by Key Books
An imprint of Key Publishing Ltd
PO Box 100
Stamford
Lincs PE19 1XQ

www.keypublishing.com

The right of Andy Brown to be identified as the author of this book has been asserted in accordance with the Copyright, Designs and Patents Act 1988 Sections 77 and 78.

Copyright © Andy Brown, 2022

ISBN 978 1 80282 212 0

Typeset by SJmagic DESIGN SERVICES, India.

Contents

Introduction

Grand Central's routes, London King's Cross to Sunderland and Bradford Interchange, run along one of the most iconic routes in Britain, the record-breaking East Coast Main Line (ECML). The company's striking black and orange livery is one of the most recognisable colour schemes on the network today.

The trains pass through scenic and interesting landscapes throughout the north of England and along the route from the capital. The North Eastern route from Sunderland takes in the Durham Coast, skirts the Cleveland Hills, passes over the flatlands of the Vale of Mowbray and onto the historic City of York. It then passes through the Vale of York itself before heading into South Yorkshire and Doncaster. The West Riding route from Bradford skirts the Valleys of West Yorkshire, threading between rivers, mills and local industry before joining the ECML at Doncaster. The two routes then combine for the fast run through the flatlands and fens of the East Midlands, Cambridgeshire, Bedfordshire and Hertfordshire and on into the capital city, London.

The book is initially split into geographical chapters for each section of the route, the North Eastern, West Riding and southern ECML. There is a chapter on trains away from the core routes, followed by unusual pictures of Grand Central trains in the 'Rarities and Maintenance' chapter, and a chapter marking the last couple of weeks of HST operation for Grand Central. The book concludes by looking at the notable changes that have been made during the last three years, including the troubles that Grand Central has experienced.

This book is a celebration of Grand Central's operation. Contributions from some of the finest railway photographers in the country enhance the collection of images, which encompass the stunning landscape of Grand Central operations throughout its first 13 years. Although a handful of locations are duplicated, I believe every shot has a relevance to the story of Grand Central.

Grand Central Railway Company Background and History

Grand Central is an open-access operator, running 18 high-speed services a day on two routes from Bradford Interchange and Sunderland to London King's Cross. In 2017, the business celebrated ten years of train operations, having initially commenced service on 18 December 2007 with one Sunderland–King's Cross and one York–King's Cross return service each day. The company continues to ignite expansion with extra services and potential new routes.

Following the delayed delivery of the six overhauled Valenta-fitted HST power cars and 18 Mk3 trailer vehicles, the full timetable of three return services from Sunderland was introduced from March 2008. After initial reliability issues, the striking black HST sets operated all Grand Central services until the first Class 180s were leased to bolster the fleet in 2009. With the Class 180s having joined the fleet, a fourth return Sunderland service was introduced the same year.

Operations on the West Riding route, from Bradford Interchange to London King's Cross, began on 23 May 2010 with three daily return services, operated exclusively by Class 180s, with the business' access rights also being extended by the Office of Rail and Road (ORR) until 2016. On only four occasions has a Grand Central HST visited Bradford Interchange, three trips having operated in passenger service, plus the 'Grand Farewell' railtour in December 2017.

In 2010, it saw the sale of the Class 43 power cars and Mk3 trailer vehicles to Angel Trains under a lease-back agreement, with the power cars being subject to re-engineering and fitment of MTU engines. During this programme, a new livery was applied to the HST fleet, with revised logos and deep orange 'swoosh' to match that applied to the Class 180 units. Grand Central operated the final Valenta-fitted power car on the ECML with some special farewell trips between York and Sunderland. 43123 received the *Valenta* name as part of this event, marking the end of over 30 years of Valenta power on the ECML.

A major change for Grand Central occurred in 2011, with acquisition by Arriva UK Trains in November of that year, and the company has operated as part of Arriva's wide European transport portfolio ever since. The December 2011 timetable change also saw Mirfield added as a station call to the West Riding service.

The timetable further expanded in 2012, with a fourth service on the West Riding route and a fifth on the North East route. This timetable has remained broadly unchanged for the last five years, with the exception of stops at the newly opened Low Moor station from early 2017, Grand Central having operated the first service to call upon opening. In 2014, the ORR granted a further access right extension until 2026.

The final Grand Central HST services ran on 31 December 2017, and from January 2018, it operated a fleet of ten Class 180 units. Having continued to succeed and grow, the business employs 222 people in London, York, Bradford and Sunderland, whilst handling 1.4 million passenger journeys per year (figures as of 2019–20).

In addition to the existing units, the cascaded Class 180s joined the refurbishment programme, which also included another subtle rebranding. A lighter shade of orange was used, and the 'by Arriva' branding was added to the Grand Central logo.

Reliability of units improved, including modifications to the Scharfenberg couplers. This meant capacity could be increased by coupling units together, and, for the first time, services were booked as ten-car trains on certain peak diagrams.

In 2019, in an industry-driven change, the first internally recruited drivers selected from the senior conductor grade commenced training, marking a new avenue of development (one already common with other operators) within the company. During 2021, Grand Central employed its first externally recruited new drivers, 'off the street'.

Grand Central was very close to expanding its sphere of operation to the West Coast Main Line. Track access rights were granted between Blackpool North and initially, Queen's Park, the last main line station north of London Euston, before the extension into the West Coast terminus was subsequently granted. The introduction of locomotive-hauled trains along the route was planned for 2020, with Class 90s and Mark 4 coaching stock cascaded from the ECML. Significant crew training took place and trains were refurbished and re-liveried in preparation of the autumn start date.

However, when the whole country was decimated by the COVID-19 virus, and with minuscule passenger numbers across the whole industry, it ultimately became unfeasible to introduce the service because of the significant risk to the whole business. With much regret, the paths were handed back to Network Rail, the rolling stock was handed back to the leasing company, and the plan was shelved.

In an act of self-protection during the COVID-19 crisis, Grand Central opted to suspend all services, and place staff on furlough for three separate periods. No trains operated from 4 April to 26 July 2020, 7 November to 2 December 2020 and 9 January to 26 March 2021. Some welcome additional revenue came during August 2020, when a crewed set was hired on weekdays to operate Leeds–Hebden Bridge shuttle services for Northern, which boosted income while passenger usage on the London-bound services remained low.

As COVID-19 restrictions were gradually lifted, passenger numbers started to increase, with some trains becoming busy, especially in the leisure sector. For the immediate future, Grand Central will be concentrating on continuing the work to keep the company stable. It will also be integrating the open-access model outlined within the new Great British Railway Williams–Shapps Plan for Rail, which promises to support and encourage new initiatives outside the franchises where spare capacity exists.

A special 10th birthday crest was fitted to the side of 43480 prior to the 'Grand Farewell' railtour on 17 December 2017. (Andy Brown)

Chapter 1
The Early Days

Grand Central obtained six HST power cars and three rakes of Mark 3 coaches to run the initial Sunderland to King's Cross services. The power cars were purchased directly from Porterbrook Leasing, and all were buffer-fitted ex-DVT test bed examples that had been overhauled at RML Services, Devonport, during 2007. The ex-loco-hauled coaches were rewired, converted to operate with HST power cars and fully refurbished.

With a scheduled start date during autumn 2007, it was necessary to train up crews on the route. Rolling stock was hired in from other rail partners in order to give route learning experience to the drivers and safety-critical on board staff. Similar Mark 3 coaches were used during these runs to familiarise crew with the stock. The training runs commenced in August 2007, and, following a lengthy repair and refurbishment period and further training and testing of the HSTs, the first Grand Central service ran on 18 December 2007.

The HST power cars needed rectification work in early 2008, which was followed by a further period of 'bedding in' for a few months, and the fleet needed support from other types of hired-in traction until they were fully ready to enter daily service later that year.

Locomotives and Mark 3 stock were hired in from Direct Rail Services (DRS) for the early crew training runs. Here, 47237 leads five DRS-liveried Mark 3a coaches, plus 47802 on the rear, as it passes Appleton Roebuck with the last 1Z43 09.06 Sunderland–King's Cross Grand Central training run on 24 August 2007. The leading cab looks quite busy, with several drivers paying close attention to the route. (Phil Chilton)

Later the same day, on the return working, the 1Z44 14.01 King's Cross–Sunderland crew training run is led by DRS' 47802 top and tailing with 47237 as it passes Dawdon with the final northbound working on 24 August 2007. (Phil Chilton)

Looking absolutely pristine on the first full main line outing for a Grand Central HST, 43080 heads south near Thirsk with 5Z00 11.45 Heaton CS–York on 8 November 2007, along with 43067 on the rear. The set had earlier worked between Heaton and Newcastle Central and back before running south along the East Coast Main Line (ECML). (Ian Ball)

43080 is again leading for another 'first' as it approaches Langford, south of Biggleswade, with the 5A60 Sunderland–King's Cross, on 9 November 2007. This was the first Grand Central HST to head into King's Cross. (Alisdair Anderson)

At a time when the availability of the HST power cars was very low, other locos and stock were drafted in to cover, and some changes were made to the timetable. For photographers, this gave the opportunity to photograph locomotive-hauled trains on the ECML. As a short-term measure, Class 67s were hired in along with Mark 2 rolling stock from EWS to cover the full King's Cross–Sunderland and return diagram. Here, 67020 leads the 1N28 16.50 King's Cross–Sunderland service past Ryther on 23 April 2008, with 67002 *Special Delivery* on the rear. (Anthony Hicks)

A month later, and the trains were hired in from another provider, as seen in this stunning view of Riviera Trains' 47805 *Talisman* leading the 1Z63 17.30 Sunderland–York service past Shippersea Bay near Easington on the glorious evening of 24 May 2008. BR Green-liveried 47815 *Great Western* is on the rear. (Neil Gibson)

XP64-liveried 47853 *Rail Express* approaches Billingham Junction with its train of maroon Mark 2 coaches forming the 1Z25 10.08 York–Sunderland on Monday 9 June 2008. 47815 is the rear loco. (Neil Gibson)

By June, the locomotive provider had changed once again, and rather than Rivera Trains providing the power, it was GB Railfreight (GBRf) subleasing some of the Thunderbird Class 57/3s from Virgin Trains. Here, 57308 *Tin Tin* skirts the Durham Coast at Dawdon with the 1Z26 14.44 York–Sunderland on 19 June 2008. 57301 *Scott Tracy* is on the back. (Neil Gibson)

This is a wider and higher view of the coast at Dawdon, and it sees 57301 *Scott Tracy* heading the 1Z63 17.30 Sunderland–York under the footbridge, while 57308 *Tin Tin* (closest to the camera) brings up the rear on 20 June 2008. (Neil Gibson)

Chapter 2

Core Routes: Sunderland to Doncaster

Grand Central's North Eastern service connects Sunderland, Hartlepool, Eaglescliffe, Northallerton, Thirsk and York with London King's Cross. This chapter covers trains and locations between Sunderland and Doncaster, with the route between Doncaster and London King's Cross being separated into a stand-alone chapter combined with West Riding services also south of Doncaster.

Photographically, it is a line of contrasts. The route starts off at Sunderland with a station wholly covered, giving the feel of being underground. Interestingly, it also shares the track with the local metro system. Once it departs from Sunderland, the line runs for a lengthy spell along the Durham Coastline, with views of the North Sea. It then heads through the industrial town of Seaham, before it quickly reaches a scenically impressive section between Dawdon and Hartlepool. This area has a number of National Trust sites, with beaches and clifftop views being especially attractive. After the line passes through Hartlepool, it heads inland and becomes industrial. Chemical plants and oil terminals quickly feature, as the line passes through the towns of Billingham and Stockton-on-Tees before arriving at Eaglescliffe. The outlook becomes far more rural in this area, with distant views of the Cleveland Hills and North Yorkshire Moors. The line remains flat, running through countryside before joining the ECML at Northallerton.

Once on the main line, line speeds increase, and trains are able to run to their full capability. Despite that, the scenes from the window and through the camera lens are generally green, with mile after mile of agriculture and fields, interspersed with the occasional village. The section between Thirsk and York is nicknamed the 'racetrack' because of its straight nature, and it has regularly been used to test the speed capabilities of various trains, including the High Speed Train/Inter-City 125 as operated by Grand Central.

Once the line crosses over the River Ouse, the train slows down for the arrival into the historic city of York, with its large curved and structurally beautiful railway station. The city is also the location of Grand Central's head office. The line heads southwest from York, and passes through an area of suburban spread, some of which is built on former railway land (at Dringhouses). It diverges from the Leeds line at Colton Junction, which was built in 1983 to take the ECML away from its previous route via Selby. The 'Selby Diversion' was built as a new part of the route to avoid an area of potential subsidence over the Selby Coalfield. It also had an additional benefit of speeding up journeys, with the original route via Selby having major speed restrictions.

The new route runs along the Vale of York, and, by its nature, passes through mainly flat rural land all the way to Doncaster. It does pass closely by two of the three Aire Valley power stations, Drax and Eggborough, both of which are highly visible from the line. On the approaches to Doncaster, it passes Shaftholme Junction, where the Askern Branch (and consequently the West Riding route) meets the ECML. As the route arrives at the station, the historic Doncaster Works, birthplace of many famous locomotives, dominates the area.

43068 brings up the rear of the 1N26 11.27 King's Cross–Sunderland as it passes Ryhope Grange on 4 March 2010. 43065 is leading, passing the signal box. The rusty lines in the foreground are the sidings at Ryhope Grange, and the line that branches off to the right in the distance is to Sunderland South Docks. The dock complex itself can be seen jutting out into the sea above the rear power car. (Andy Brown)

180105 still carries the original First Great Western livery as it passes Dawdon on 4 March 2010, with the 1A62 12.30 Sunderland–King's Cross. The unit had been recently transferred over to Grand Central, and it retained the old livery until the end of May the same year. (Andy Brown)

Carrying the original plain black Grand Central livery, 43065 heads north along the Durham Coast at Dawdon with the 1N26 11.27 King's Cross–Sunderland on 2 March 2010. The rear power car is 43084. (Neil Gibson)

With the bodywork looking typically sparkling, 180105 *The Yorkshire Artist Ashley Jackson* passes Dawdon on 10 March 2015 with the 1N92 11.21 King's Cross–Sunderland. (Steve Bennett)

During the winter months, the landscape around the railway becomes brown and yellow, as the old foliage and grasses die back. Nowhere is this more evident than on the top of the exposed Durham Coast cliffs, as can be seen here with 43084 passing Dawdon on 17 January 2009. The working is the 1A62 12.30 Sunderland–King's Cross, and on the rear is 43067. The line of bushes above the third coach marks the route of the branch to Dawdon Colliery, which closed in 1991. (Ian Ball)

Taken from more or less the same spot as the previous image, a much more lush and green summer landscape is seen, including lots of wildflowers. 43123 leads the 1A61 14.32 Sunderland–King's Cross past Dawdon on 8 August 2010, with 43084 on the rear. (Jason Cross)

A beautifully colourful image in stunning December light sees the final version of the Grand Central black with orange stripe livery on 43423 *Valenta 1972-2010*, lit to perfection as it leads 43468 on the 1A65 12.28 Sunderland–King's Cross past Dawdon on 3 December 2014. This location is often referred to locally as 'Blast Beach', and an area of the beach at the foot of the cliff in the background was a former waste coal dumping site, now happily cleaned up and a National Trust beauty spot. (Jonathon Kirby)

43480 negotiates the gentle s-curves as it leads 43465 past Hawthorn Hive with the 1A65 12.28 Sunderland– King's Cross service on 26 February 2016. (Ian Ball)

In a beautiful scene featuring late spring flowering gorse bushes, immaculate 43465 leads 43480 past Shippersea Bay, Easington, with the 1A61 08.42 Sunderland–King's Cross service on 26 May 2014. (Ian Ball)

43484 *Peter Fox 1942-2011* approaches Hart Station on 10 March 2015 with the 1N93 12.53 King's Cross–Sunderland. 43423 *Valenta 1972-2010* is on the rear. The train is rounding the curve that was formerly the site of the junction with the line to Haswell, and which followed the straight alignment to the right of the HST. In the background can be seen the urban and industrial sprawl of Hartlepool. (Steve Bennett)

In a view photographed at the exact point of the junction of the closed line to Haswell, and the remaining line to Sunderland via the coast, 43484 *Peter Fox 1942-2011* is again the subject of the shot on the rear of the 1A65 12.28 Sunderland–King's Cross on 18 November 2016. 43465 is the leading power car. In this unusual view, the greenery of the golf club contrasts with the deep blue of the North Sea. Steetley Pier is in the background. (Ian Ball)

With a shortage of serviceable HST power cars, Grand Central 'hired in' 43304 from Arriva CrossCountry to bolster the fleet for a short time. It is seen rounding the curve at Hartlepool on the rear of the 1N90 07.51 King's Cross–Sunderland. 43480 is leading and rounds the curve on 25 February 2014. (Michael J Alderdice)

43123 approaches the semaphore signal at Billingham Junction with the 1N25 07.57 King's Cross–Sunderland on 10 May 2008, along with 43080 on the rear. (Neil Gibson)

43484 *Peter Fox 1942-2011* leads six Mk3s and 43423 *Valenta 1972-2010* as the 1A69 Sunderland–London King's Cross makes steady progress towards the capital, seen passing Hartburn Junction on 19 July 2016. (Jonathon Kirby)

With a wave from the driver, the 1A69 17.31 Sunderland–King's Cross is seen passing the Moorhouse Estate, on the approach to Eaglescliffe on 28 August 2017. 43465 leads the set, with 43423 *Valenta 1972-2010* on the rear. The train is seen gathering speed, having passed over a long-standing 20mph speed restriction at Stockton Cut Junction. Of note is the strengthened formation of this Grand Central HST set (GC02), running in 2+8 formation in place of the usual 2+6. An additional TSD and TSO have been added to the set to provide extra capacity for various events over the bank holiday weekend. A second set, GC01, was also strengthened in a similar fashion. (Jonathon Kirby)

43480 leads GC03, tailed by 43484, as the 1A69 17.31 Sunderland–London King's Cross and is seen passing Brompton foot crossing on the approach to its next station call, Northallerton, on 30 June 2015. (Jonathon Kirby)

43467 fronts 43484 *Peter Fox 1942-2011* as it approaches Brompton foot crossing with the 1N90 08.02 King's Cross–Sunderland on 19 April 2017. (Ian Ball)

180105 *The Yorkshire Artist Ashley Jackson* works the 1A60 06.45 Sunderland–King's Cross as it heads along the up slow line past South Otterington on a lovely clear 10 August 2015. The farm in the background is called Station Farm, so chosen as the old Otterington railway station is immediately behind the photographer. (Jonathon Kirby)

43084 leads the 1A60 06.53 Sunderland–King's Cross as it passes the iconic 'Edinburgh 200 Miles' London North Eastern Railway (LNER) sign next to Overton Road bridge, Shipton-by-Beningbrough, on 8 August 2009. The rear power car is 43123. (Dave Stacey)

By mid-afternoon, the shot becomes nicely sunlit on the other side of the line from the previous image. 43423 *Valenta 1972-2010* passes the other 'Edinburgh 200 Miles' sign at Shipton-by-Beningbrough on the 1A65 12.28 Sunderland–King's Cross on 10 May 2017. (Tom Robson)

43480 pilots the 1A65 12.28 Sunderland–King's Cross through the countryside near Overton on 11 December 2017 in sparkling winter sunshine, assisted from the rear by 43423 *Valenta 1972-2010*. (Andy Brown)

Looking a little more weather beaten than normal, thanks to passing over track that had recently been treated with sandite for leaf fall, the first Grand Central livery adorns 43067 and the full rake, including 43084 on the rear, as it arrives at York station on 6 December 2008 with the 1A62 12.30 Sunderland–King's Cross. (Neil Harvey)

43068 sends a big plume of exhaust smoke into York station roof as the driver opens it up to depart from Platform 5 with the 1N26 11.27 King's Cross–Sunderland on 2 April 2010. Less than a month later, this power car was one of the first two to head to Brush Works in Loughborough for its MTU engine conversion. (Neil Gibson)

Recently overhauled and re-engineered with an MTU power unit, 43480 pauses at York on the rear of the 5N28 19.24 Peterborough–Heaton Traction & Rolling Stock Maintenance Depot (T&RSMD) empty coaching stock (ECS) on 11 October 2010 after the set failed earlier in the day. The HST is being hauled by 67029 (out of sight on the front), which was coupled up to 43123. As part of the conversion work, the power car and the Mark 3 trailers had recently also been repainted and branded with the new orange stripe version of the Grand Central livery. (Andy Brown)

43480 is in charge of the 2+6 Grand Central HST on the 1A61 08.42 Sunderland–King's Cross as it passes the site of Chaloners Whin Junction on 12 September 2017. 43467 is the back power car for this service. Around the position of the white streetlights at the back of the train, the original trackbed of the ECML one diverged, heading south via Selby. That line was closed and replaced by the present 'Selby Diversion' alignment via Hambleton when the Selby Coalfield was opened in 1983. (Andy Brown)

In lovely evening light, 43465 leads 43467 towards Beckett's Crossing, Copmanthorpe, on 12 June 2014, with the 1A69 17.31 Sunderland–King's Cross. (Neil Harvey)

42423 *Valenta 1972-2010* speeds past the site of the closed station at Copmanthorpe with the 1N90 08.03 King's Cross–Sunderland on 17 August 2017. 43465 is tucked away on the back. (Andy Brown)

43480 heads the 1A60 09.20 Sunderland–King's Cross through the classic scene at Colton Junction on 26 November 2017, along with 43484 on the rear. (Kieren Cross)

43467 passes Colton Junction on the lovely sunny evening of 9 May 2016 at the head of the 1A69 17.31 Sunderland–King's Cross. 43465 is on the back. (Andy Brown)

In the similar stance to the previous picture and the same leading power car, but in its previous Valenta-powered guise, 43067 heads the 1A63 17.30 Sunderland–King's Cross at Colton with 43080 at the back on 30 May 2009. (Andy Brown)

Valenta-powered 43123 heads the recently converted MTU-engined 43468 as they approach Colton Junction amid fine autumn colours with the 1N25 08.04 King's Cross–Sunderland on 30 October 2010. (Neil Harvey)

The two brown cows seem to be untroubled by the sound of 43467 leading the 1A60 09.20 Sunderland–King's Cross through Appleton Roebuck, just south of Colton Junction, on 23 October 2016, with 43480 on the rear. (Andy Brown)

43467 disturbs the rural peace as it heads north between Bolton Percy and Appleton Roebuck (known to local photographers as 'Bridge 33') on the approach to Colton Junction. It is running a couple of minutes early with the 1N94 16.50 King's Cross–Sunderland on 8 July 2013. 43465 is the back power car. (Andy Brown)

As harvest time approaches, 43123 heads south past Thorpe Willoughby with the 1A60 06.41 Sunderland–King's Cross on 1 August 2008. (Neil Gibson)

The striking foreground of the oilseed rape field contrasts with 43123 as it speeds past Thorpe Willoughby with the 1A60 06.46 Sunderland–King's Cross on May Day, 1 May 2009. (Neil Gibson)

43080 leads a 2+5 HST formation as it passes Thorpe Willoughby and approaches Hambleton South Junction with the 1N28 16.50 King's Cross–Sunderland on 7 May 2009. 43084 is the back power car. (Andy Brown)

A picture taken in the interim period between the original plain black livery and that with the orange stripe sees 43468, newly converted with an MTU power unit, leading an otherwise full original-liveried black rake on the 1A62 12.30 Sunderland–King's Cross passing Gateforth on 7 October 2010. Valenta-powered 43123 is on the rear.

During the winter when we are lucky enough to get some snowfall, locations are transformed, as seen here in this view of 180112 *James Herriot* forming the 1A60 09.10 Sunderland–King's Cross as it passes Gateforth on 5 December 2010. (Anthony Hicks)

43480 leads the 1A65 12.28 Sunderland–King's Cross Grand Central service past Lunds Farm at Gateforth on 22 February 2016. The rear power car on this occasion is 43465. (Andy Brown)

As usual, looking as fresh as the day the set emerged from the paint shop, 43465 passes Burn on the 1N94 16.50 King's Cross–Sunderland on 30 April 2015. 43467 is the back power car. (Neil Gibson)

This stunning profile scene captures the grace and speed of 43423 *Valenta 1972-2010* leading the 1A69 17.31 Sunderland–King's Cross as it passes Burn on 23 April 2015. (Neil Gibson)

43465 on the front and 43484 on the back pass Burn with the 1A65 12.28 Sunderland–King's Cross Grand Central service on 6 October 2016. Judging by the clouds, getting this shot in sun was quite fortunate. (Andy Brown)

43423 *Valenta 1972-2010* and 43468 throw up the lying snow as they pass a wintry Burn on 5 February 2012, with the 1A60 09.13 Sunderland–King's Cross. (Andy Brown)

43123 is seen at the head of the 1N26 11.27 King's Cross–Sunderland as it passes Burn on 8 December 2010. Just visible at the rear beside the trees is a recent MTU conversion, 43468. (Neil Harvey)

In a reversal of the previous shot, the front power car is in the original livery, with the remainder of the train having been refreshed into the new orange stripe version of the Grand Central livery. Lit by only hazy sunshine, Valenta-fitted 43084 screams past Burn while heading a full train in the new livery with orange stripe; it is tailed by 43480 as it works the 1N26 11.27 King's Cross–Sunderland on 2 October 2010. (Andy Brown)

In rather a classic view of ECML activities, and a much nicer one when fully lit by the late spring sunshine, 43423 *Valenta 1972-2010* passes Burn at line speed with the 1N94 16.50 King's Cross–Sunderland on 13 May 2014. Drax Power Station can just be seen at the top left of the shot, on what appears to be a rather still evening. (Neil Gibson)

Looking like the meat in a colourful sandwich, 43468 (on the left of the picture) leads 43484 *Peter Fox 1942-2011* along the banking at Heck on 5 November 2014 with the 1A61 08.42 Sunderland–King's Cross. (Sam Middleton)

43467, leading the 1A61 08.30 Sunderland–King's Cross Grand Central service, passes Joan Croft on 9 August 2014 with 43480 on the back. (Andy Brown)

180112 *James Herriot* passes Joan Croft with the 1A66 15.18 Sunderland–King's Cross on 24 September 2014. (Neil Gibson)

Chapter 3

Core Routes: Bradford Interchange to Doncaster – West Riding

Grand Central's West Riding service connects Bradford Interchange, Low Moor, Halifax, Brighouse, Mirfield, Wakefield Kirkgate, Pontefract Monkhill, and Doncaster with London King's Cross.

The route starts at the relatively new station of Bradford Interchange, which was built on the approaches to the previous, and much grander, Bradford Exchange. The new station is of 1970s architectural design, and the 'Interchange' also has the large adjoining bus station, hence the name, which was changed from the original 'Exchange' in 1983.

The line from Bradford immediately climbs a steep incline and soon passes through the first of six tunnels, the 1,648-yard-long Bowling Tunnel, which is the longest on the entire route to London King's Cross. A consequence of the undulating landscape, with its high tree-lined cuttings, is that it is difficult to photograph this section of line.

Trains call at the new Low Moor station, and once the line emerges from Beacon Hill Tunnel, they arrive at Halifax station. The town still houses some industry, with factories visible from the station itself. There is a heritage feel to the town, with many of the closed mills converted to a variety of museums, art galleries and centres of interest. The recently refurbished Piece Hall is a highlight. Once the line departs from Halifax, it heads once again downhill and into the eastern extremities of the Calder Valley towards Elland, Brighouse and Mirfield, with views of the river along with the Calder & Hebble Navigation canal.

The route to Wakefield is a mixture of rural landscapes and industrial backdrops at various stages. The sad decline of the once-thriving Healey Mills railway yard is evident as the West Riding service passes on opposite sides of the former freight hub, depending on the direction of travel.

The train calls at the recently refurbished and much-improved Wakefield Kirkgate station, and after departure the route diverges. Some Grand Central services continue along the Leeds–Doncaster main line, whereas others head along the former Lancashire and Yorkshire route towards Pontefract Monkhill. The route features a mixture of residential, industrial and rural interludes.

Pontefract is a market town of historic interest. The castle can be seen from the train, along with scars of industry: the mass spoil heap of the former colliery is also visible but is now undergoing redevelopment for housing.

Once the train departs from Pontefract, the immediate area is dominated by the remaining vast cooling towers of the now-closed Ferrybridge power station. The line south from Knottingley was closed to passengers in 1948, until the Grand Central service once again restored the line to passenger-carrying status in 2010. The route is largely rural and flat, with little in the way of landmarks, although it passes through the small spa town of Askern. This section of line is often referred to as the 'Askern Branch'. The branch joins the ECML at Shaftholme Junction, and the main line heads south for the short distance into Doncaster.

180112 *James Herriot* has just arrived at its destination with the 1D73 14.48 King's Cross–Bradford Interchange on 15 September 2017. It is seen in Platform 2 at Bradford Interchange. (Andy Brown)

180101 passes Mill Lane Junction on the approaches to Bradford Interchange with the 1D93 15.50 King's Cross–Bradford Interchange on 6 July 2014. On this day, the Tour de France, which had commenced in Yorkshire the previous day, passed through Hebden Bridge and Huddersfield, and several extra trains had been laid on to take spectators to and from the event. (Andy Brown)

Above: 43423 *Valenta 1972-2010* glints as it leads set GC03 and 43468 with the 5A83 09.25 Doncaster–Bradford Interchange ECS past Mill Lane Junction on the approaches to Bradford Interchange station on 28 December 2014. The diagram for both Saturday and Sunday of that weekend saw this set working from Sunderland before reversing at Doncaster for the empty stock to Bradford. (Andy Brown)

Right: 180107 is about to enter Beacon Hill Tunnel, Halifax, with the 1D75 14.20 King's Cross–Bradford Interchange on 24 May 2010. This was during the first week of the service between Bradford and London. (Neil Harvey)

180112 *James Herriot* passes through Halifax and is about to enter Beacon Hill Tunnel with the 5A63 08.40 Crofton Depot–Bradford Interchange ECS on 9 August 2012. The unit would then continue its diagram by forming the 1A63 10.21 Bradford–King's Cross. (Rob Whitaker)

In a stunning picture of a train in its surroundings, 180107 *Hart of the North* calls at Halifax station on 1 September 2017 with the 1A63 10.21 Bradford Interchange–King's Cross. (Neil Harvey)

180112 *James Herriot* departs from Halifax station on 6 June 2014 with the 1D73 14.48 King's Cross–Bradford Interchange service. (Andy Brown)

180114 passes Dryclough Junction with the 1A74 15.33 Bradford Interchange–King's Cross on a sunny 23 May 2010, the very first day of Grand Central operation in the West Riding. (Anthony Hicks)

180107 approaches Brighouse with the 1A73 12.08 Bradford Interchange–King's Cross on the very first day of the service operating on 23 May 2010. (Anthony Hicks)

On the second occasion a Grand Central HST set worked a West Riding service, 43468 approaches Brighouse with the 1A83 11.17 Bradford Interchange–Finsbury Park on 28 December 2014. The first occasion is documented later in the book. (Anthony Hicks)

43468 makes a fine sight as it passes Heaton Lodge Junction with the 1A83 11.17 Bradford Interchange–Finsbury Park on a wintry 28 December 2014. (Neil Gibson)

180101 approaches Mirfield with the 1A74 15.22 Bradford Interchange–King's Cross service on 2 April 2011. The vantage point for this shot is the bridge that formerly led to the engine shed at Mirfield. (Gavin Morrison)

180112 James Herriot departs from Mirfield with the 1D71 10.48 King's Cross–Bradford Interchange on 30 March 2012. The train is passing the site of Mirfield Engine Shed, which is now occupied by the modern housing behind the railway. (Neil Harvey)

180112 *James Herriot* forms the 1A63 10.21 Bradford Interchange–King's Cross over the point work at Mirfield East Junction on 21 April 2016. (Sam Middleton)

43468 makes for a marvellous sight as it passes a wintry-looking Healey Mills with the 1A83 11.17 Bradford Interchange–Finsbury Park on 28 December 2014. The rear power car is 43423, and the set is GC03. Trains were stopping short of King's Cross over the Christmas Bank Holiday weekend due to engineering work. (Andy Brown)

180101 threads along Horbury Cutting as it is captured from Addingford Lane Bridge with the 1A83 12.04 Bradford Interchange–King's Cross on 10 June 2012. (Gavin Morrison)

180112 *James Herriot* threads through Horbury Cutting under a dramatically moody sky with the 1A63 10.21 Bradford Interchange–King's Cross on 29 July 2015. (Sam Middleton)

180105 passes Millfield Lane, Horbury, with the 1A63 10.22 Bradford Interchange–King's Cross on 3 June 2010. (Gavin Morrison)

180114 passes Featherstone while working the 1D71 10.48 King's Cross–Bradford Interchange on 22 February 2016. The background might benefit from a little greenery! (Andy Brown)

Class 180 no 180105 passes the site of the original Pontefract Tanshelf station with the 1A75 10.22 Bradford Interchange–King's Cross on 1 March 2011. (Andy Brown)

43465 arrives at Pontefract Monkhill bang on time with the 1D71 10.48 King's Cross–Bradford Interchange on 17 July 2012. The unusual use of an HST on the West Riding service was to check clearances at stations along the route – this was also the very first time a Grand Central HST had been used in service along the whole of the West Riding route. 43467 is the back power car. (Andy Brown)

On a day of diversions and service alterations, owing to engineering work on the Leeds to Doncaster main line, 180102, on short-term hire and still in the original ex-First Great Western livery, passes Pontefract East Junction with the 1A81 09.35 Bradford Interchange–Doncaster service on 22 April 2012. (Andy Brown)

A month after the previous shot was taken, 180105 *The Yorkshire Artist Ashley Jackson* passes an avenue of hawthorn blossom at Pontefract East Junction working the 1A63 10.22 Bradford Interchange–King's Cross on 22 May 2012. Please forgive the indulgence of two shots at the same location – it was at that time the closest location to the photographer's house! (Andy Brown)

180112 *James Herriot* eases round the curve at Knottingley on 17 April 2012 with 1A63 10.22 Bradford Interchange–King's Cross. The industrial backdrop is dominated by Ferrybridge power station. (Andy Brown)

180101 approaches Seniors Bridge, just south of Knottingley, with the 1A63 10.22 Bradford Interchange–King's Cross on 16 November 2010. Ferrybridge power station, in the left background, is working hard on the cold winter day, with steam rising up from the cooling towers. The former Rockware Glass factory (now Aardah Glass) sits immediately in front of the power station in this scene. (Anthony Hicks)

180101 heads along the Askern Branch line and approaches Norton on 1 May 2015 with the 1A67 14.33 Bradford Interchange–King's Cross. (Rob Whitaker)

There are two routes used by Grand Central between Wakefield Kirkgate and Doncaster. Some trains run via the old Lancashire and Yorkshire route to call at Pontefract Monkhill and turn south via the Askern branch line, while others head via the faster, more direct Leeds to Doncaster main line through South Elmsall. Here, 180105 *The Yorkshire Artist Ashley Jackson* passes through Bentley Station, just north of Doncaster, on the latter route with the 1A83 12.05 Bradford Interchange–King's Cross on 27 January 2013. (Anthony Hicks)

From the change of timetable in May 2016, a Grand Central Class 180 and its crew were utilised by Arriva Trains Northern to strengthen their morning peak service from Bradford Interchange to Leeds. This was further enhanced from the December 2016 timetable change, when the service started from Halifax, providing the daily view of a Grand Central unit into one of the busiest stations in the country. Here, 180112 *James Herriot* has just arrived at Platform 6 in Leeds, right in the middle of the busy morning peak and going unnoticed by the hundreds of commuters heading to work, having arrived with the 2T99 07.44 Bradford Interchange–Leeds on 15 November 2016. The next working for the unit is the 5T99 08.40 Leeds–Bradford Interchange ECS, followed by the 10.21 Bradford–King's Cross. (Andy Brown)

To complete the West Riding selection, here are a couple of rarely seen in-cab views of the HST in the West Riding. These shots were taken on the gauging trial of 17 July 2012, and Driver Team Manager (DTM) Simon Rudge is seen at the controls of 43465 as it passes through Elland, working the 1D71 10.48 King's Cross–Bradford Interchange. (Rob Whitaker)

The second in-cab shot shows DTM Simon Rudge easing the train down the descent into the platform at Bradford Interchange as it finally arrives with the 1D71 10.48 King's Cross–Bradford Interchange on 17 July 2012. Sadly, on only three more occasions would a Grand Central HST make it to Bradford Interchange, twice on a service train and once on the 'Grand Farewell' railtour during their final weeks of operation for the company. (Rob Whitaker)

Chapter 4

Core Routes: Doncaster to London King's Cross – ECML Southern Section

Both of Grand Central's core routes, the North Eastern Sunderland to King's Cross and the West Riding Bradford Interchange to King's Cross, converge at Doncaster and head south on the famous ECML to London.

Both sets of services run directly with no station stops, but they pass through towns such as Retford, Newark, Grantham, Peterborough, Huntingdon, Stevenage, and the North London suburbs before arriving at the 1852-built former Great Northern Railway terminus at King's Cross.

The direct nature of the North Eastern service between York and London means that Grand Central offers some of the fastest journey times between the two, with some trips arriving in less than two hours. The West Riding service runs with no station stops between Doncaster and London, and it too has the fastest journey times between the two points, with certain services timed in under 1hr 40min.

The route is generally quite flat with only gentle curves, enabling regular line speeds of 125mph. Once out of the towns and cities, it is very rural in appearance until the North London suburbs are reached. The line passes various landmarks, with Lincoln Cathedral being visible to the east on a clear day. Other places of interest include Peterborough Cathedral, Arsenal's football ground, the Emirates Stadium, and Alexandra Palace. The line also runs over Stoke Bank, which is famous as the location where, in 1938, A4 Class no 4468 *Mallard* set the world speed record for the fastest steam locomotive at 126mph, a record that still stands today.

This chapter covers selected locations along the route that have a relevance to Grand Central's trains.

180101 speeds through the centre road at Doncaster with the 1A60 06.45 Sunderland–King's Cross on 21 March 2017. (Andy Brown)

43080 passes Doncaster Down Decoy Yard with the 1N26 11.27 King's Cross–York on 5 January 2008. 43068 is on the rear. Unusually, the five-coach rake includes one standard class coach, one buffet car and three first-class trailers! (Andy Brown)

180101 (with its coupler cover still in place) emerges from Pipers Wood, just north of Bawtry, working the 1A59 06.55 Bradford Interchange–King's Cross on 11 June 2011. (Steve Bennett)

43084 heads away from Eaton Lane Level Crossing at speed on 3 February 2009 while on the back of the 1N25 08.04 King's Cross–Sunderland service. 43080 is on the front, out of sight and round the curve. (Jason Cross)

43465 emerges from Askham Tunnel as it leads the 1N94 16.48 King's Cross–Sunderland on 9 August 2014. On the rear, still inside the tunnel, is 43484. (Phil Chilton)

Recognisable by the sun-bleached orange Grand Central logos, 180101 speeds round the curve at Tuxford on 1 July 2014 with the 1A67 14.20 Bradford Interchange–King's Cross. (Andy Brown)

43468 powers the 1N94 16.48 King's Cross–Sunderland past some stunning colour at Carlton-on-Trent on 22 May 2012 ably assisted from the rear by 43423 *Valenta 1972-2010*. (Rob Whitaker)

43468 and 43480 are paired up as they form the 1A60 06.45 Sunderland–King's Cross at Cromwell on 18 April 2017. Even the nicely tailored field to the right of the line is noteworthy with the juvenile crops. (Jonathon Kirby)

Even after harvest time, the same field as the previous image remains well-tailored. 180107 *Hart of the North* is seen at Cromwell on 1A81 07.55 Bradford Interchange–King's Cross on 24 September 2017. This scene is an example of how lovely the colours in the railway landscape can be. (Kieren Cross)

43480 flies through North Muskham on 13 June 2017 at the head of the 1N94 16.50 King's Cross–Sunderland with 43468 on the rear. The location is just north of Bathley Lane Level Crossing. (Jason Cross)

180105 *The Yorkshire Artist Ashley Jackson* has just passed through Newark North Gate station and speeds towards the flat crossing with the 1D81 16.03 King's Cross–Bradford Interchange on 25 May 2014. (Sam Middleton)

43467 approaches the popular photographic location of Balderton Level Crossing, just north of Claypole Loop, with the 1N94 16.50 King's Cross–Sunderland on 15 August 2017. 43468 is the rear power car. This crossing, which carries Broad Fen Lane over the line, is midway between the villages of Balderton and Claypole and is most recognisable by the farm buildings tucked up close to the line. (Kieren Cross)

43484 *Peter Fox 1942-2011* speeds towards Balderton crossing with 1N94 16.50 King's Cross–Sunderland on 5 May 2017, along with 43468 on the back. Although this is the same location as the previous image, a different outlook is provided by the camera being in an elevated position. (Andy Brown)

180107 *Hart of The North* passes the village of Hougham on 5 May 2017 with the 1D81 16.03 King's Cross–Bradford Interchange. This unit was named following a 'Name Our Train' competition in the *Hartlepool Mail*. Jack Sharp, 15, from Hartlepool came up with the name, which he said, 'showed the warmth of the people in Hartlepool', and he unveiled the nameplate on 24 October 2010 at London King's Cross. (Jason Cross)

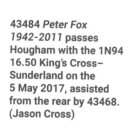

43484 *Peter Fox 1942-2011* passes Hougham with the 1N94 16.50 King's Cross–Sunderland on the 5 May 2017, assisted from the rear by 43468. (Jason Cross)

The colourful oilseed rape crops really stand out within the landscape in late April and early May, which rewards photographers with vivid colours for a short time. A classic example can be seen here, as 43468 passes Frinkley Lane, just north of Peascliff Tunnel, with the 1A65 12.28 Sunderland–King's Cross on 5 May 2017. 43484 is the rear power car. (Kieren Cross)

In a typical ECML-style view, 43423 *Valenta 1972-2010* heads the 1N94 16.50 King's Cross–Sunderland past Frinkley Lane on 4 August 2017. This has the addition of the '40 Years 1976|2016' crest below the nameplate, which is to commemorate 40 years of HST operation. The power car on the back on this occasion is 43465. (Rob Whitaker)

43484 *Peter Fox 1942-2011* speeds through Grantham station on 5 December 2015 with the 1N94 16.48 King's Cross–Sunderland. Modern digital cameras and clever photographic techniques enable images such as this, where the train is captured travelling at line speed at night-time. (Jason Cross)

180114 heads along the up fast line at Little Ponton on 12 June 2010 with the 1A59 06.51 Bradford Interchange–King's Cross. The nearest track is the slow line, which provides a passing loop for traffic south of Grantham to just north of Stoke Tunnel. The flowers add some colour to the deep green height of summer landscape. (Jason Cross)

Back to the early plain black era once again, and here we see 43068 tailing 43067 as they pass Little Ponton with the 1N25 07.57 King's Cross–Sunderland on 25 July 2009. The train is made up of five coaches, which were strengthened as the stock passed through works in the following months. (Phil Chilton)

It was less common during the later years for a shortened Grand Central HST rake to be formed. Here, 43484 *Peter Fox 1942-2011*, it's five coach rake and 43423 on the back, emerge from Stoke Tunnel at High Dyke with the 1N93 King's Cross–Sunderland on 22 July 2012. (Ian Holmes)

We move now to the southern end of the ECML, and a sparkling 43468 is seen approaching Biggleswade with the 1A60 06.45 Sunderland–King's Cross on 21 September 2010. This is the first outing for the power car following its re-engineering with an MTU engine, and it has received a full repaint into the revised orange stripe version of the Grand Central livery. It contrasts with the remainder of the train, which is in the original plain black livery. (Alisdair Anderson)

180112 passes through Biggleswade on 29 July 2009 with the 1Z61 09.18 Sunderland–King's Cross VIP special to celebrate a significant occasion, the first working of a Grand Central-liveried Class 180 into London. The unit looks pristine, having been delivered fresh from repaint at Wolverton Works only four days previously. In addition, this celebrated the start of the fourth Sunderland to King's Cross and return paths. On arrival at King's Cross, the unit was named *James Herriot*, after the famous North Yorkshire vet and author, by Jim Wight and Rosie Page, son and daughter of Alf Wight, the vet and author who created the James Herriot character. (Alisdair Anderson)

43480 works the first service train operated by an MTU power car for Grand Central, seen here in lovely light as it passes Langford on 18 September 2010 with the 1A60 06.45 Sunderland–King's Cross. The trailer cars had recently been rebranded at Kilmarnock Works and are seen to great effect. The rear power car is Valenta-fitted 43084, still in the original black livery. (Alisdair Anderson)

43484 passes Langford, on the rear of the 1N90 07.49 King's Cross–Sunderland on 19th May 2011. The power car has absolutely spotless paintwork, as it had been named *Peter Fox 1942-2011* (after the railway publisher) at Sheffield a week beforehand. 43467 is the power car on the opposite end of the train. (Alisdair Anderson)

180107 *Hart of the North* passes Great Wymondley, between Hitchin and Stevenage, as it works the 1A63 10.21 Bradford Interchange–King's Cross on 6 November 2017. (John Turner)

With a lovely view of southern ECML architecture and infrastructure, 43484 *Peter Fox 1942-2011* emerges from Welwyn North Tunnel with the 1A65 12.28 Sunderland–King's Cross service on 2 March 2015. 43423 is on the back, just inside the tunnel mouth. (Rob Whitaker)

180114 *Kirkgate Calling* runs amongst early autumn colour as it passes Welham Green working the 1A63 10.21 Bradford Interchange–King's Cross on 31 October 2017. (John Turner)

180107 *Hart of the North* heads north on the 1D73 14.48 King's Cross–Bradford Interchange as it passes Ganwick on 10 March 2015. Just out of shot on the left are the twin bore entrances to Potters Bar Tunnel. (Rob Whitaker)

Into the North London suburbs, and 43480 dodges the winter sunshine shadows as it leads the 1A61 08.42 Sunderland–King's Cross through Alexandra Palace on 8 December 2017, assisted from the rear by 43423. (Andy Brown)

On the left is 180107 *Hart of the North*, having arrived at King's Cross with the 1A59 06.55 Bradford Interchange–King's Cross, and on the right is newly transferred 180108, which had arrived on the 1A60 06.45 Sunderland–King's Cross. The latter remained in First Great Western livery for a further month before it was called to Eastleigh Works for a protracted refurbishment. The blue unit went on to form the 1D71 10.48 King's Cross–Bradford Interchange. Normally, these turns are out and back, where 1A59 forms 1D71, and the second unit is on the Sunderland diagram. However, on 7 July 2017, a set swap was required to get the ex-First Great Western unit onto the West Riding diagram as soon as possible. (Andy Brown)

Chapter 5

Off the Beaten Track

To quote a well-used railway adage: from time to time, it is necessary to carry out weekend engineering work! This type of maintenance results in closure of the normal route, and the solution to keep trains running is to divert them around the affected area on other lines. Featured in this chapter are images of Grand Central trains in rarer locations on some of those diversionary routes.

Amongst the routes featured include the maze of lines to the south of York, the Great Northern and Great Eastern Joint Railway through Lincoln, and the lines towards the Fens and Cambridge to the south and east of Peterborough. Also included are some locations outside their normal sphere of operation, where Grand Central trains have visited in exceptional circumstances.

180114 passes a snow-covered Hill End at Armley on 17 January 2016 with the diverted 1A83 12.05 Bradford Interchange–King's Cross. This is a well-used diversionary route for Grand Central services on a Sunday if engineering work is taking place anywhere between Bradford and Wakefield Kirkgate. Trains run from Bradford towards Leeds as far as Whitehall Junction, where they then reverse and travel to Wakefield Kirkgate via the Great Northern Leeds to Doncaster main line through Wakefield Westgate and round the curve into Kirkgate. (Anthony Hicks)

180101 is well off the beaten track, as it is seen here having just departed from Selby en route to Hull. The unit is in fact on hire to Hull Trains, and it eases up to the signal at a snowy Barlby with the 1H02 10.45 King's Cross–Hull on 5 February 2012. (Andy Brown)

180112 *James Herriot* has just run along the Goods Line and departs from Derby station on 14 September 2014 with the rather circuitous 5Z81 09.32 Heaton T&RSMD– Longsight Carriage Maintenance Depot via Nuneaton empty coaching stock. The unit is heading to the Manchester depot for tyre turning. The famous Derby Works clock tower dominates the skyline. (Anthony Hicks)

43484 *Peter Fox 1942-2011* leads 43467 past Winwick, near Warrington, working the 5Z43 16.03 Crewe CS–Heaton T&RSMD empty stock on 5 April 2012. Grand Central services should have been passing this location on a daily basis on the now-cancelled Blackpool North and London Euston service, via the West Coast Main Line (WCML). (Terry Eyres)

43084 leads 43067 as it approaches Norton West Junction with the diverted 1A60 09.10 Sunderland– King Cross on 23 May 2010. (Ian Ball)

Although only just 'off the beaten track', as the line it would normally take can be seen in the top right of the shot, 43480 and 43467 work the diverted 1A61 08.08 Sunderland–King's Cross on a very wintry 26 January 2013, as it passes Colton South Junction. This route is used when the ECML is closed between York and Doncaster, and on this particular day would head to Doncaster via Milford Junction, Castleford, the outskirts of Wakefield and South Elmsall. (Anthony Hicks)

43080 looks clean in the plain black original Grand Central livery as it takes the Castleford (up Normanton) line passing Milford Junction. The working is the diverted 1A60 09.10 Sunderland–King's Cross on the sunny morning of 5 April 2009. 43084 is the rear power car. (Andy Brown)

43480 snakes across Milford Junction while working the 1A60 09.20 Sunderland–King's Cross on 17 April 2016, along with 43465 on the back. The diversion route for this train is via Burton Salmon, Ferrybridge and the Askern Branch. (Anthony Hicks)

Diverted due to engineering work between York and Hambleton North, 43465 leads the 1A60 09.43 Hartlepool–King's Cross past Burton Salmon, along with 43480 on the back, on 16 March 2014. (Andy Brown)

43067 leads the diverted 1A60 09.10 Sunderland–King's Cross with 43068 on the back past a very snowy-looking Burton Salmon on Easter Sunday, 23 March 2008. (Andy Brown)

43065 contrasts with the laying snow as it leads the diverted 1N25 08.55 King's Cross–Sunderland through Burton Salmon, with 43084 on the back, on Easter Day, 23 March 2008. The diversion would take the train off the ECML and run via the Askern Branch, Ferrybridge and Milford. (Andy Brown)

43465 passes through the village of Burton Salmon, where the lines from York to Castleford and Ferrybridge diverge. In days gone by, this was quite a busy location, with a junction and a station serving the village. On 27 January 2013, this HST passed through just before sunset on the 1N92 13.50 King's Cross–Sunderland. 43484 is on the back. (Anthony Hicks)

43068 approaches Fairburn Tunnel with the diverted 1N25 09.35 King's Cross–Sunderland on 5 April 2009. 43123 brings up the rear. Again, the diversion route for this particular day was via South Elmsall, Normanton and Milford Junction. Fairburn Ings Nature Reserve dominates the background. (Andy Brown)

43080 leads the diverted 1A60 09.10 Sunderland–King's Cross as it negotiates the complex and slow running section of line between Knottingley station and Knottingley marshalling yard on 21 September 2008. 43068 is the rear power car. The service was diverted via Milford Junction and Ferrybridge, and the location in this picture is the start of the Askern Branch south to Shaftholme Junction, where it joins the ECML. (Neil Gibson)

On 5 April 2009, 43068 heads the diverted 1N25 09.35 King's Cross–Sunderland past the site of the Welbeck spoil disposal point near Normanton, which is seen behind the train. 43065 is the back power car. Just behind the photographer is the site of Goose Hill Junction, where the line previously diverged to Crofton and the closed Midland Main Line via Cudworth. The flat ballast in the foreground was the original track bed for that route. On the distant hill side, is the Emley Moor transmitter, which can be seen for miles around the entire South and West Yorkshire area. (Neil Harvey)

On 16 October 2010, 43123, on the rear of the 1A62 12.30 Sunderland–King's Cross, is seen diverted via Lincoln, with refurbished MTU-fitted 43468 at the front. The train is crossing Sincil Bank Level Crossing. The tightly curved line to the left heads out towards Barnetby and Grimsby. The piece of land immediately above the rear power car was the site of Lincoln Traction Maintenance Depot, which closed in the late 1980s. The old engine shed still stands and can be seen as the grey building with the pointed roof and clock on the peak, which is now used as a bus depot. (Andy Brown)

Six weeks or so before the end of HSTs at Grand Central, 43423 *Valenta 1972-2010* leads 43468 on the 1A60 09.20 Sunderland–King's Cross past Washingborough on 12 November 2017. This lovely scene is dominated by Lincoln Cathedral, which sits proudly on the hillside. On a clear day, the cathedral can be seen from the ECML, which was closed on the day of this shot, hence the diversion via Gainsborough, Lincoln and Sleaford. (Anthony Hicks)

43484 *Peter Fox 1942-2011* passes Metheringham with the 1A60 09.45 Hartlepool–King's Cross on 5 November 2017. On the rear is power car 43465. This was a planned diversion, due to engineering work on the ECML between Newark North Gate and Peterborough. (Kieren Cross)

On a beautifully sunny day, 43480 heads south near Quadring with the diverted 1A60 09.20 Sunderland–King's Cross on 19 November 2017. This village is midway between Sleaford and Spalding on the former Great Northern and Great Eastern Joint Railway (the 'joint line'). The back power car is 43484. (Kieren Cross)

43480 and 43423 *Valenta 1972-2010* pass Lattersey Hill at Whittlesea as they work the diverted 1A65 13.20 Northallerton–King's Cross, running 78 minutes late, on 4 February 2017. There are two spellings of the place Whittlesea. In this caption, I have used the older railway spelling, but outside the railway it is spelt 'Whittlesey'. (John Turner)

180101 passes Oldeamere, working the diverted 1N93 12.20 King's Cross–Sunderland on 4 February 2017. Engineering work was taking place north of Hitchin on the ECML, hence the diversion via the Fens. (John Turner)

43484 *Peter Fox 1942-2011* and 43465 pass Turves with the diverted 1A61 08.30 Sunderland–King's Cross on 4 February 2017. (John Turner)

43065 and 43067 pass Westry on the approach to March with the diverted 1A60 06.53 Sunderland–Cambridge Grand Central service on a misty 21 March 2009. (John Turner)

43067 and 43065 pass March West Junction, having just passed through the Fenland market town's station with the diverted 11.25 Cambridge–Sunderland Grand Central service on 21 March 2009. (John Turner)

Chapter 6

Rarities and Maintenance

rains break down, just like anything mechanical. Moving parts wear out and require regular maintenance. In this chapter, there are images of Grand Central trains that are receiving assistance, under test or moving to depots for maintenance work, together with behind-the-scenes shots not normally seen by passengers travelling around the railway network.

An extremely rare working shows Grand Central HST power car 43067 on 28 September 2008 at Bishop Wood, on the Selby diversion section of the ECML, leading the Network Rail New Measurement Train (NMT) on the 5Z69 15.48 Newcastle–Doncaster. This working was to accumulate miles for the recently overhauled Valenta Paxman power unit. It made a further run that day and completed the runs fault free. The power car on the back is 43062 *John Armitt*. (Andy Brown)

Earlier on the same day as the previous shot, 43067 rounds the curve at Gateforth with the first of two high speed runs, the 5Z67 12.30 Heaton T&RSMD–Doncaster, on 28 September 2008. (Ian Ball)

In order to accumulate 'problem-free' mileage, Grand Central's 43067 was given a run out with a scratch rake of stock and 47375 dead on the rear from Heaton to Taunton on 29 September 2008. However, a late departure from Heaton saw the schedule amended to run as far as Bristol East Depot. 43067 and 47375 pass Portway in poor light on 29 September 2008 with the 5Z67 11.35 Heaton Traincare Depot–Bristol East Depot. In the end, the train only ran as far as Gloucester Horton Road before being turned on the Gloucester triangle and returning to Derby. (Scott Borthwick)

Colas Railfreight's 47739 *Robin of Templecombe* heads a rather colourful consist past Hunslet on 10 April 2010. This is the 5Z43 12.45 Neville Hill T&RSMD–Heaton Traincare Depot ECS, conveying two Porterbrook barrier vehicles and two Grand Central HST coaches that had been to the Leeds depot for attention. (Andy Brown)

An unusual working sees Thunderbird 67029 *Royal Diamond* in the special EWS Manager's silver livery at York with a failed 43084 on 11 October 2010. The consist forms the 5N28 19.24 Peterborough–Heaton T&RSMD ECS and 43484 was on the back (out of sight). The set sat in the station for nearly two hours, having lost its path owing to other delays, and later formed the re-timed 5N28 23.00 York–Heaton T&RSMD. (Andy Brown)

Although the weather is not the sparkling light that railway photographers prefer, the rarity of Arriva CrossCountry's 43384 tailing 43480 on the 1A65 12.28 Sunderland–King's Cross is worthy of inclusion. The multi-coloured train arrives at Hartlepool on 11 February 2014. (Michael J Alderdice)

These types of workings always raise an eyebrow as they are relatively few and far between. 43423 *Valenta 1972-2010* passes Raskelf light engine as the 0Z43 07.00 Heaton T&RSMD–Crewe L&NWR on 14 April 2014. The power car was heading to Crewe for cab refurbishment work. (Ian Ball)

Europhoenix-liveried 37800, on hire to the Rail Operations Group, scores a very rare working indeed, as it drags a full Grand Central HST set, led by 43480 and tailed by 43423, past Gateforth on the 5A12 13.44 Bounds Green T&RSMD–Heaton T&RSMD on the lovely, sunny evening of 12 April 2017. (Andy Brown)

Usually out of sight, and carrying out its business unnoticed, immaculately painted in Grand Central livery, RMS Locotec-owned 08648 *Amanda* basks in the sunshine on the fuel road at Heaton Traincare Depot on a sweltering 19 July 2016 as it awaits its next shunting duty. (Andy Brown)

08648 *Amanda* and 43480 sit inside the main shed at Heaton Traincare Depot on 1 December 2017. (Jason Rogers)

08648 *Amanda* and an unidentified Class 180 Adelante DMU sit inside the main shed at Heaton Traincare Depot on 6 February 2017. (Jason Rogers)

It was a day of celebration when the open day took place at St Phillips Marsh HST depot in Bristol on 2 May 2016. It marked the 40th birthday of the most iconic diesel train ever to run in the UK, the High Speed Train, known as the Inter-City 125. First Great Western special-liveried 43172 *Harry Patch* stands beside Grand Central's 43423 *Valenta 1972-2010*, Network Rail's NMT power car 43013, Virgin Trains East Coast's 43300 *Craigentinny* and East Midlands Trains' (EMT) 43048 *T.C.B. Miller MBE.* (Kieren Cross)

A multi-coloured HST lash-up sees Virgin Trains East Coast's 43300 *Craigentinny* leading Network Rail's 43013, Grand Central's 43423 *Valenta 1972-2010*, the preserved prototype 41001 and its stock, and tailed by EMT's 43048 *T.C.B. Miller MBE* passing Lea Marston with the 5Z43 06.20 St Phillips Marsh HSTD–Derby Etches Park ECS on 3 May 2016. The cavalcade had been on display at the Bristol depot the previous day as a celebration of 40 years of the HSTs. (Andy Brown)

A joint exercise was arranged between Grand Central, Hull Trains and Network Rail on 29 January 2018 to revise and practise locomotive assistance procedures for failed Class 180s. The exercise took place at Heaton Depot, utilising Arriva blue-liveried LNER Thunderbird 67003, which was hired for the purpose. Here, the loco and the simulated 'failed' Class 180 are seen successfully coupled and brake tested on Line B within the depot. (Jonathon Kirby)

On 22 July 2018, 180104 failed at Biggleswade with an electrical fault whilst working the 1D95 19.22 King's Cross–Bradford Interchange. Clearing the line involved a move at 5mph to Langley Lafarge Siding, hauled by 180103. Traffic requirements for the aggregate terminal meant a further move was required later in the week to Hitchin Down Yard (via Hertford North to run round), hauled by LNER Thunderbird 67014. Final recovery to Crofton was arranged for the early hours of 2 August. Rail Operations Group provided 37608 to haul the errant unit as the 7Z18 01.45 Hitchin Down Yard–Crofton Depot via the GNGE Joint Line. The route prevented running over the lengthy sections of two-track ECML at 40mph. The Class 37 and unit are seen here in Hitchin Down Yard, just prior to departure. (Jonathon Kirby)

Chapter 7

Ten Years On: Farewell to the HSTs

On 18 December 2007, the first Grand Central service operated using the iconic HSTs, the Inter-City 125. These high-quality trains gave ten years sterling service to Grand Central, and it was with some regret amongst crews that the use of these trains ended. In the final months of service, they became a high priority of the railway landscape photographer on the ever-changing list of desirable subjects. In this chapter, shots are featured from the final few days.

The 'Grand Farewell' railtour took place on 17 December 2017, worked by a Grand Central HST and crew to mark the end of their operation. The tour ran in association with the Branch Line Society, the 125 Group and other railway partners, and raised a significant sum to benefit railway charities. The tour worked along some of the core routes operated by Grand Central, together with other much rarer lines where Grand Central trains are most unusual. The itinerary even included track that sees no passenger trains at all.

The official end date of Grand Central's HST operation was 31 December 2017, and also featured in this chapter are pictures of the final week of operation, between Christmas and New Year, including the very last diagrams on the final day.

With specially painted silver buffers complementing the shiny bodywork, 43423 *Valenta 1972-2010* sits at Newcastle Central station early on 17 December 2017 at the rear of the 1Z41 08.05 Newcastle–Doncaster Roberts Road Shed. This was the first part of 'The Grand Farewell' tour, which would also run via Sunderland, Barrow Hill, the Hope Valley line, the Calder Valley line, Gascoigne Wood and York. The occasion marked the end of Grand Central's HST operation, together with the 10th birthday of the operator. (Andy Brown)

While on the high-speed ECML, the tour was banned from having its 'The Grand Farewell' headboard fitted. Once the train headed along the slower routes, it could be refitted. During a pause in proceedings, 43480 sits at Sheffield Midland before taking the next leg of the tour forward, the 1Z42 11.55 Doncaster Roberts Road Shed– Barrow Hill South Junction. 43423 is the rear power car. (Andy Brown)

With its headboard fitted, there was time for a photo call at Sheffield. 43480 is featured and beside the power car is a line-up of the volunteers on the train. Representatives from Grand Central, the Branch Line Society, the 125 Group, Network Rail, Direct Rail Services, and the Railway Children Charity can be seen, including the author at the front left. (Anthony Hicks)

Following a leisurely trip over the Calder Valley line, 43423 *Valenta 1972-2010* leads the 1Z43 13.25 Barrow Hill South Junction–Bradford Interchange leg into Bradford Interchange just after 16.30 on 17 December 2017. This would be the very last Grand Central HST to depart from Bradford Interchange, led by 43480, which in this shot is on the opposite end of the train. (Kieren Cross)

43423 *Valenta 1972-2010* is seen at the front of the 1Z44 16.36 Bradford Interchange–Newcastle via Gascoigne Wood Down Goods Loop 'The Grand Farewell' railtour as it is about to depart from York on 17 December 2017. The back power car is 43480, out of sight round the curve. (Tom Robson)

The day after the 'Grand Farewell' railtour, 18 December 2017, 43484 *Peter Fox 1942-2011* takes a turn to share the limelight and carries the tour headboard during a brief photo opportunity while being serviced at Heaton Traincare Depot. 43468 is at the other end of the train. (Jonathon Kirby)

With only a handful of days left in Grand Central squadron service, 43465 is captured calling at York with the 1A69 17.31 Sunderland–King's Cross on 27 December 2017. 43467 is out of sight on the rear. (Steve Bennett)

With Bishop Wood behind the train, 43465 leads the 1A65 12.28 Sunderland–King's Cross over Selby Dam Viaduct, just north of Hambleton North Junction, on 28 December 2017. 43467 is on the rear. (Neil Gibson)

Although the sunlight could have been a bit stronger, 43480 still carries its silver buffers from the 'Grand Farewell' railtour as it leads the very last southbound Grand Central HST service, the 1A61 12.12 Sunderland–King's Cross on New Year's Eve, 31 December 2017. 43467 is the partner on the rear, matching the very first two power cars to work for Grand Central ten years earlier. The train is crossing the River Wharf Viaduct at Ozendyke, one minute before 14.00. (Andy Brown)

Fittingly, in a burst of lovely winter sunshine, 43480 and 43467 are photographed rounding the curve on the approach to Askham Tunnel with the 1A61 1212 Sunderland–King's Cross on 31 December 2017. (Phil Chilton)

Chapter 8

2018 to 2021:
Continuing the Voyage

With Grand Central's HST fleet now transferred to franchise operator East Midlands Trains (EMT), the Grand Central Class 180 fleet size doubled to ten units, with the addition of five former First Great Western units to replace the HSTs. The units were refurbished at Eastleigh Traincare Depot. Practical training became an important element for staff development. The use of the one-and-a-half-mile-long Hendon branch between Ryhope Grange Junction and Sunderland Docks by Grand Central crews for low-speed handling and coupling training was of huge benefit. Owing to its proximity to Crofton Depot, where the Class 180 fleet is serviced, the Monk Bretton branch is also being assessed for other training.

Training also became an important part of the plan for Blackpool North–London Euston services. The introduction of Class 90s and Mark 4 coaching stock cascaded from the ECML was an exciting development, and trains were refurbished and re-liveried in advance.

During the COVID-19 crisis, Grand Central opted to protect itself by suspending all services and placing staff on furlough for three separate periods. Sadly, this also saw the demise of the Blackpool–London plan. Some financial respite came when Grand Central operated Leeds to Hebden Bridge shuttle services for Northern.

Going forward, Grand Central will be continuing work to keep the company stable, assuming a 'business as usual' approach to keep the company on a firm footing, with further development when the time is right.

In the final chapter, we look at images of some of the changes that occurred during turbulent times for the whole industry.

Stock Changes

The start of a New Year, but the end of an era. The lease ended on the Grand Central HSTs at midnight on 31 December 2017, going on to EMT. Shorn of all logos, set GC03 is led by a similarly de-branded 43465 as it passes Burton Salmon with the 5A17 07.42 Heaton CS–Neville Hill T&RSMD in the first of the year's sunshine, at just after 9.00 on 1 January 2018. On the rear, 43484 still carries the Grand Central logo, but not the *Peter Fox 1942-2011* nameplates. (Andy Brown)

Former First Great Western Class 180s were cascaded to Grand Central, with 180108 initially bolstering the fleet from 12 May 2017. At the start of 2018, the rest of the Great Western units were transferred to Grand Central to replace the HSTs. 180108 still looks mint in the blue 'swoosh' livery, as it speeds north past Shipton on 25 June 2017 with 1N94 16.48 King's Cross–Sunderland. *(Jason Rogers)*

Refurbishments were carried out at Eastleigh Traincare Depot, with the blue units being the priority over the existing black and orange sets. Before being called into works, the blue trains served Grand Central well for much of 2018. 180103 passes Thornes, having just left Wakefield Kirkgate, with the 1D71 10.48 King's Cross–Bradford Interchange service on 5 April 2018. (Andy Brown)

Refurbishment

As well as an internal refit, with new seating, carpets and buffet counter, the units received a full repaint in a modified version of the Grand Central black and orange house colours. A lighter shade of orange was used for the stripe, and the branding amended to include the words 'by Arriva', bringing into line the open-access operator with DB-owned franchise operations. Recently refurbished, 180112 *James Herriot* heads through the colourful countryside towards Askham Tunnel with the 1D81 16.27 King's Cross–Bradford Interchange on 15 May 2019. (Andy Brown)

180101, recently outshopped from Eastleigh Works, passes Burn on the 1A66 15.30 Sunderland–King's Cross service just before teatime on 27 June 2019, much to the delight of the author's son. (Andy Brown)

180104 passes Daw Lane Level Crossing, just south of Shaftholme Junction, with the 1A61 08.42 Sunderland–King's Cross on 23 September 2019. (Andy Brown)

Crew Training

The one-and-a-half-mile-long Hendon branch between Ryhope Grange Junction and Sunderland South Dock saw rare first use by Grand Central for low-speed driver handling and coupling training. 180103 is seen at the site of the former Hendon Junction, the limit of Network Rail infrastructure, during a traction training session on 12 March 2021. The unit had arrived on the branch as the 5N80 08.05 Heaton T&RSMD–Hendon No 1 Siding. Behind the train, and on Port of Sunderland infrastructure, the line descends through an s-bend and into a deep cutting, prior to emerging onto the quayside at Sunderland South Dock. (Jonathon Kirby)

Under menacing skies on 12 March 2021, 180103 stands having just passed over Bluehouse Subway, ready to draw up towards the exit Stop Board to gain permission to return onto the main line as 5N81 15.40 Hendon No 1 Siding–Heaton T&RSMD following traction training. Above the train, Sunderland South Dock can be seen, and in the distance in the middle of the image, it is possible to make out the breakwaters at Wearmouth. (Jonathon Kirby)

For another driver training session, the trainees practised coupling a locomotive to a stricken unit with the emergency coupler. During the exercise, we see DRS' Class 57/0 57002 *Rail Express* coupled to unit 180102 at the entrance to Londonderry Sidings, near Hendon, on the Sunderland South Dock branch on a cloudy 19 March 2021. A second Class 180 can be seen in the extreme distance, at the far end of the sidings. (Jonathon Kirby)

The Hendon branch saw further use on 6 June 2021, this time for locomotive coupling refresher training. GBRf's 60021 *Penyghent* was borrowed from the Tyne Dock biomass circuits and is seen with 180101, close to Bluehouse Subway, having been successfully coupled. The 60 arrived on the branch as the 0Y80 09.40 Tyne Dock–Hendon No 1 Siding, returning later as the 0N81 15.30 Hendon No 1 Siding–Tyne Dock. (Alex Cooke)

Blackpool to Lockdown City

The first Mark 4 coaches were transferred to the North West in batches during February and March 2020, with the first two sets being moved as one combined train, and subsequent sets being moved individually. 66750 *Bristol Panel Signal Box* and 66722 *Sir Edward Watkin* head past Clegg Hall on 6 March 2020 with the 08.59 Doncaster Works Sidings–Crewe CS, conveying the fourth Grand Central set. (Mark Delaney)

With preparations underway for the start of the Blackpool to Euston services, Grand Central staff training commenced at Wembley Yard, for which two Class 90s and a rake of Mark 4 stock were provided. EWS-liveried 90020 *Collingwood* is attached to the ex-Virgin Trains East Coast-liveried stock on 9 February 2020. (Will Etherington)

Mark 4 DVT 82228 is seen at Wembley Yard on 9 February 2020 for staff traction training, while DB-liveried 90019 *Multimodal* is stabled beside it to be used by Grand Central later. (Will Etherington)

Following a period of prolonged rainfall in the North West, 90019 *Multimodal* (coupled to Mark 4 DVT 82231) is reflected in the localised flooding as it powers the 3K83 11.51 Blackpool North–Crewe CS, just east of a now-sunny Kirkham and Wesham on the 6 March 2020. The train is top and tailed with 90036 *Driver Jack Mills*. (Jamie Squibbs)

EWS-liveried 90039 stands at the buffer stops at Blackpool North, having arrived with the 3P51 09.14 Crewe S–Blackpool North crew training run on 11 March 2020. Two trips were made during the day, this one being the first. (Will Etherington)

Its former Virgin Trains East Coast livery looking a little weather worn, Mark 4 DVT can be seen in Platform 6 at Blackpool North, with the iconic skyline, dominated by Blackpool Tower, providing the backdrop. Once the trainee drivers change ends, it will go on to form the 3K83 11.50 Blackpool North–Crewe CS on 11 March 2020. (Will Etherington)

With its WCML heritage making it look very much at home under the spacious train shed at Preston station, 90039 is solely providing power from the rear of the 3K84 16.18 Blackpool North–Crewe CS on 16 March 2020. (Will Etherington)

Sunshine lights the scene nicely as 90039 passes Moore on the approach to Acton Grange Junction as it powers the 3P51 09.19 Crewe CS–Blackpool North on 20 March 2020. (Tom Swift)

Obeying government COVID-19 guidelines, people simply stopped travelling on trains. This had serious implications for all train operators, especially the self-funding open-access operators like Grand Central. On 22 March 2020, the day before Prime Minister Boris Johnson announced to the country that they *must* stay at home, 180102 eases into Mirfield station with the 1D91 11.52 King's Cross–Bradford Interchange. The train was almost empty, and no passengers joined or alighted. Just 12 days later, Grand Central stopped running trains to protect the company, apart from the occasional stock move, and placed staff on furlough. (Andy Brown)

With train services not operating due to lockdown, opportunities were taken to carry out maintenance during their hibernation period. It was also a chance to use the couplers. Numerically last and first units, 180114 and 180101, head past the site of Goose Hill Junction near Normanton with 5N14 11.07 Doncaster Roberts Road Shed–Heaton T&RSMD on 8 May 2020, following a session on the wheel lathe for tyre turning at the South Yorkshire depot. 180114 still has a 'non-multi' sticker in place, which means the coupler on the leading end is out of action on this occasion. (Chris Davis)

By the time the lockdown had taken hold, all training on the Blackpool service was paused owing to the social distancing guidelines, and the project was delayed until early 2021. Nevertheless, the Mark 4 coaches were refurbished and repainted into Grand Central livery at Alstom's Widnes Technology Centre and the locos at Toton TMD. Breaking cover for the first time, 90026 and 90020 power away from Weaver Junction with the 5Z90 17.30 Widnes Alstom–Wembley InterCity Depot (ICD), formed of two Grand Central liveried rakes (GC04 and GC01), on 7 August 2020. (Alan Hart)

90026 leads sister 90020 and sets GC04 and GC01 over Dutton Viaduct on 7 August 2020 with the 5Z90 17.30 Widnes Alstom– Wembley ICD, where the sets were being taken for further storage, pending the restart of crew training. (Terry Eyres)

90026 and 90020 create a uniform image as they pass Acton Bridge working the 5Z90 17.30 Widnes Alstom– Wembley ICD on 7 August 2020. (Neil Harrison)

Grand Central services returned to existing core routes on 26 July 2020, initially with light loadings. Additionally, Grand Central supplied a Class 180 and crews to operate a two-hourly Hebden Bridge to Leeds service for Northern on weekdays between 27 July and 12 September 2020. 180102 is seen ready to depart from the attractive Hebden Bridge station on 21 August 2020 with the 1T28 13.43 Hebden Bridge–Leeds. (Will Etherington)

After the COVID-19 restrictions rendered plans to introduce the loco-hauled Blackpool–London Euston unfeasible, with huge regret, on 9 October 2020, the project was officially shelved. Despite being refurbished to a high standard, the Mark 4 stock never carried fare paying passengers under the Grand Central umbrella, although they were purchased by Transport for Wales and will see use along the North Wales Coast in the future. 90020 is seen coupled to 82227 and a set of Grand Central Mark 4s at Wembley Yard on 9 November 2020, with 90029 also stabled at the end of the siding pending developments. A somewhat dark end to what would have been a photogenic operation for years to come. (Richard Dyke)

Modern photography technology continues to improve and enables scenes such as these to be captured. With train services not operating due to lockdown, the sets were given warm store mileage accumulation runs during their hibernation period. One such working was captured after dark with clever use of artificial lighting, as 180106 and 180102 form a ten-car train seen heading through Horbury Cutting with the 5Z80 23.19 Bradford Interchange–Crofton Depot just after midnight on 20 May 2020. (Night Light Group)

A similar working took place in the North East on 9 June 2020, as 180108 and 180112 (out of sight on the rear) are captured passing Hawthorn Quarry on the Durham Coast line with the 5N98 22.06 Heaton T&RSMD–Sunderland via Dinsdale accumulation run. (Night Light Group)

The third return to passenger service traffic after lockdown was on 26 March 2021. 180108 sits in Platform 10 at King's Cross with the 5Z71 10.48 King's Cross–Bradford Interchange on the previous day, while Grand Central was operating empty trains in their normal paths for crew refamiliarisation. During the King's Cross station remodelling in spring 2021, the suburban platforms were rationalised, with Platforms 9 and 11 being re-laid, but Platform 10, as seen in this shot, not so. The previous Platform 11 was then renumbered to 10. (Will Etherington)

After Grand Central

The buffer-fitted former Grand Central HSTs became known as the 'Angel Sets', as they were leased to EMT by Angel Trains rather than Porterbrook Leasing, which supplied the rest of the EMT fleet. An alternative version of EMT livery is seen adorning 43480 *West Hampstead PSB* as it heads the 5C52 12.16 Nottingham–Sheffield under the conveyer at the closed Attenborough Cement Works on 17 April 2019. On the rear is 43467, another former Grand Central power car. (Andy Brown)

Grand Central-liveried Class 90s, albeit with logos removed, continue in service in the DB Cargo core fleet. 90026 double heads with Malcom-liveried 90024 past Yealand as they power the 4M25 07.07 Mossend Euroterminal–Daventry International Railfreight Terminal intermodal on 5 May 2021. (Phil Metcalfe)

Adorned in shiny black and orange Grand Central livery, 90026 leads the Malcolm-liveried 90024 at Castle Hill, Abington, with a late running 4M25 07.07 Mossend–Daventry intermodal train on 5 May 2021. (Ian Ball)

47813 *Jack Frost* makes for a fine sight as it passes Rushey Sidings west of Retford on 25 February 2021 working the 5Q26 06.53 Eastleigh Works–Worksop Sidings with the de-branded ex-Grand Central Mark 4s. The livery of the coaches is shown up favourably in this scene. Hopefully, they will enter service on the Welsh services for a time in these colours, enabling more pictures in future. (Steve Bennett)

With life gradually returning to normal as COVID-19 restrictions were being lifted, the trains returned to the rails, and a period of warm sunny weather also brought out the photographers. 180104 speeds past North Muskham with the 1N94 16.25 King's Cross–Sunderland on 20 May 2021. (Jonathon Kirby)